Third Eye

Light
Wisdom
Perception
Insight
Spirituality
Vision
Awareness

Intuition
Imagination
Indigo
Mind's eye
Ajna
Inner knowing
Enlightenment

Third Eye Chakra Adventures:

Illuminating
with
Tanzanite and Indigo

Volume 6

By: K.C. Gold

"This book is dedicated to you.
Look beyond your horizon."

Northern Lights Publishing LLC.

https://northernlightskids.com/

Hello, I'm Tanzanite, and Indigo's my friend, Spinning energy particles where intuition begins.

We are between your eyebrows, we have an iridescent glow,
They call us Third Eye Chakra, so now you know.

We guide your imagination
with radiant light,
Nurturing your intuition
from morning to night.

We love to have fun and assist when it's due,
But sometimes we need help, that's true.

If your mind's eye dims

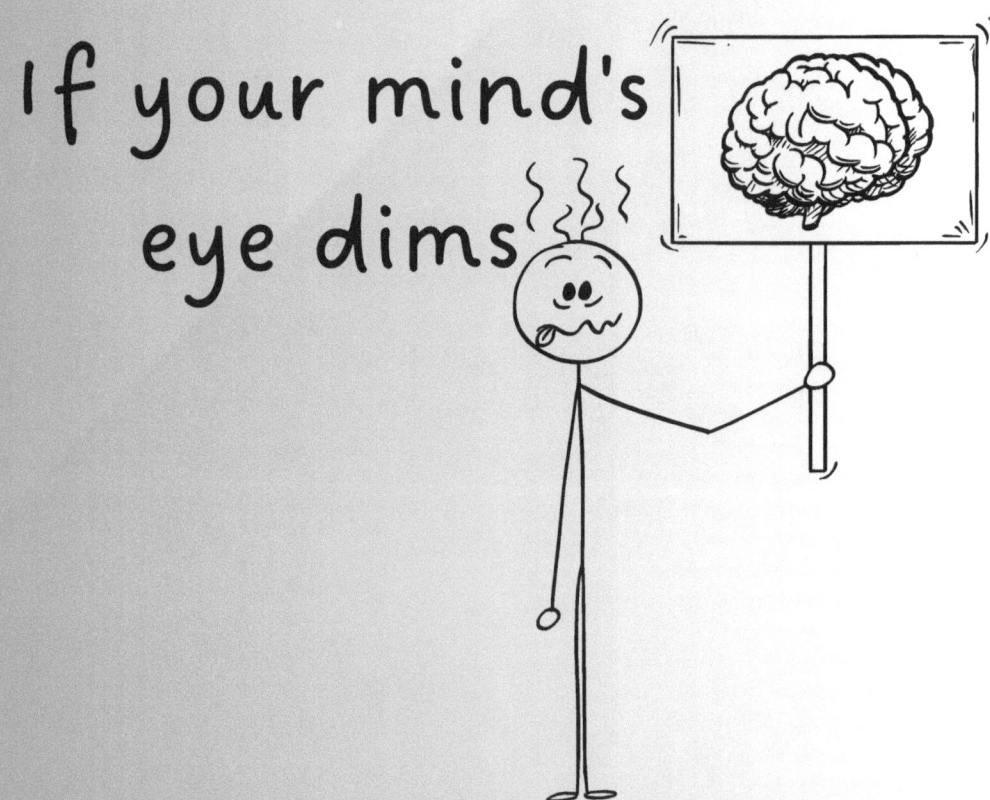

And your intuition starts to cry,

A veil descends upon you,
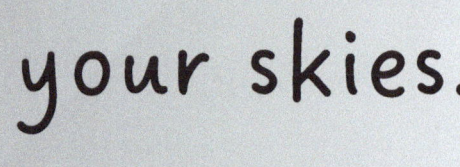 obscuring
your skies.

It means we are
blocked
and
unbalanced,
it's true.

But there are many things
you can do,
To get us spinning back
around 852 times, plus two.

Hertz Meter

1 Hertz (Hz) = 1 Spin Per Second

852Hz

Sweet sounds delight us, 'A' pitch we adore,
With its melody so pure, our spirits start to soar.

Dance and sway your head,
watch us start to twirl,
In a vibrant indigo swirl, we
start to spin and whirl.

Dress in shades of blue, as deep as the sea,
In harmony with nature, is where you're meant to be.

Enjoy a treat from the Earth, where nourishment is found,
Delicious and blue, let its taste astound.

Do what you need, we're here to guide you through, And when you find a quiet place, here are some mantras for you:

"I trust my insight like a guiding star, Intuition leads me, near and far!"

"Present in the moment, like an owl so keen,
Observing, learning, in every scene."

"The wisdom of the universe flows through me,
Guiding me on my journey!"

"I trust my instincts, like a detective's clue, Seeing clearly, I know just what to do!"

Feel your energy rising as we spin and move,
Dancing in this wonderful world of blue hues.

Through cosmic waves, we'll
guide your sight,
Awaken your Third Eye, lift
the veil with light.

Third Eye
Light
Wisdom
Perception
Insight
Vision
Spirituality
Awareness

Dear Reader,

Thank you for taking the time to read this book. If you found value in it, I would be incredibly grateful if you could take a few moments to leave a review. Your feedback not only helps me improve but also aids other readers in discovering books they might enjoy.

Thank you once again for your support and for being a part of this adventure!

Warm regards,
K.C. Gold

Amazon

Northern Lights Publishing

Look beyond your horizon.

www.ingramcontent.com/pod-product-compliance
Lightning Source LLC
Chambersburg PA
CBHW041434120626
46547CB00002B/205